S0-AIC-957

GREAT CITIES
OF THE WORLD

CAIRO

South Huntington Pub. Lib.
145 Pidgeon Hill Rd.
Huntington Sta., N.Y. 11746

ROB BOWDEN AND ROY MACONACHIE

WORLD ALMANAC® LIBRARY

916.216
Bowden

Please visit our web site at: www.worldalmanaclibrary.com
For a free color catalog describing World Almanac® Library's list of high-quality books and multimedia programs, call 1-800-848-2928 (USA) or 1-800-387-3178 (Canada). World Almanac® Library's fax: (414) 332-3567.

Library of Congress Cataloging-in-Publication Data

Bowden, Rob.
    Cairo / by Rob Bowden and Roy Maconachie.
      p. cm. — (Great cities of the world)
    Includes bibliographical references and index.
    ISBN 0-8368-5035-1 (lib. bdg.)
    ISBN 0-8368-5195-1 (softcover)
    1. Cairo (Egypt)—Juvenile literature. I. Maconachie, Roy. II. Title.
III. Series.
    DT143.B69   2004
    962'.16—dc22   2004041939

First published in 2005 by
World Almanac® Library
330 West Olive Street, Suite 100
Milwaukee, WI 53212 USA

Copyright © 2005 by World Almanac® Library.

Produced by Discovery Books
Editor: Kathryn Walker
Series designers: Laurie Shock, Keith Williams
Designer and page production: Keith Williams
Photo researcher: Rachel Tisdale
Diagrams: Keith Williams
Maps: Stefan Chabluk
World Almanac® Library editorial direction: Mark J. Sachner
World Almanac® Library editor: Gini Holland
World Almanac® Library art direction: Tammy West
World Almanac® Library graphic design: Scott M. Krall
World Almanac® Library production: Jessica Morris

Photo credits: AKG Images/Gilles Mermet: p. 20; AKG Images/Tony Vaccaro: p. 13; AKG Images/Ullstein: pp. 12, 14; Corbis: pp. 8, 11, 22; Corbis/Tom Nebbia: p. 36; Corbis/K.M. Westermann: p. 16; Corbis Sygma/Neema Frederic: p. 18; Easi-Images/Rob Bowden: p. 30; Easi-Images/Roy Maconachie: pp. 4, 7, 17, 19, 21, 24, 25, 27, 28, 29, 31, 33, 34, 37, 39, 42, 43; Still Pictures/Sean Sprague: p. 38; Still Pictures/Hjalte Tin: p. 32; Trip/D. Harding: cover and title page; Trip/Brian North: pp. 10, 23; Trip/J. Pilkington: p. 40

Cover caption: Shoppers browse in a traditional bazaar, or market, in one of Cairo's older districts.

All rights reserved. No part of this book may be reproduced, stored in a retrieval system, or transmitted in any form or by any means, electronic, mechanical, photocopying, recording, or otherwise, without the prior written permission of the copyright holder.

Printed in the United States of America

1 2 3 4 5 6 7 8 9 08 07 06 05 04

Contents

Introduction

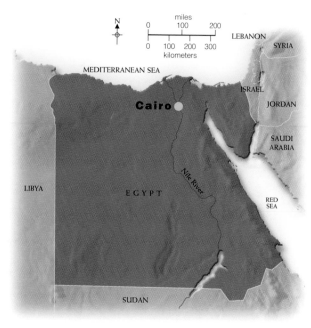

Cairo is the capital of Egypt and one of Africa's greatest cities. Once the center of the Ancient Egyptian civilization, it is now the most populous city in Africa. Cairo is the educational, political, and cultural center of the Arabic-speaking world. Home to the oldest Islamic universities, some of the world's finest mosques, and the Arab League (a cooperative organization of twenty-one Arabic countries), Cairo also produces most of the Arabic movies.

◀ *The minarets of Cairo's ancient mosques provide a dramatic contrast to the modern offices and hotels of the city center.*

From the Cairo Tower, a modern 614-foot (187-meter) structure in the center of the Nile River, it is possible to view five thousand years of history. To the west, new suburbs sprawl outward until they meet the ancient pyramids that tower majestically above them. To the southeast lie the Citadel (the fortified royal city of Cairo's past rulers) and the vast Muslim cemeteries known as the Cities of the Dead. More immediately east, the central business district of Cairo displays its modern offices, government buildings, and international hotels.

Many Cities in One

Cairo is a city of great diversity and enormous contrasts. It is often thought of as many cities in one. In the oldest parts of Cairo, such as Al-Qahirah, it feels as though time has stood still. Al-Azhar university first opened its doors in A.D. 970, and Khan al-Khalili market has been busy with traders for about seven hundred years. These oldest parts of the city have changed little over the centuries. The more modern

"He who hath not seen Cairo hath not seen the world: her soil is gold, her Nile is a marvel . . . her houses are palaces; and her air is soft . . . rejoicing the heart. And how can Cairo be otherwise when she is the Mother of the World?"

—Anonymous, *The Thousand and One Nights*, date unknown.

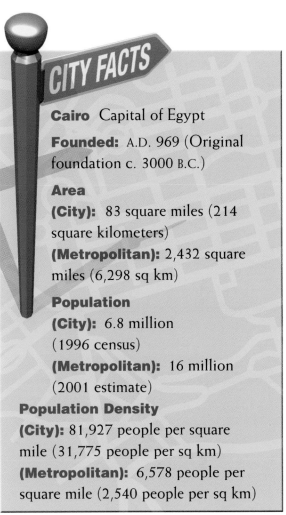

CITY FACTS

Cairo Capital of Egypt

Founded: A.D. 969 (Original foundation c. 3000 B.C.)

Area
(City): 83 square miles (214 square kilometers)
(Metropolitan): 2,432 square miles (6,298 sq km)

Population
(City): 6.8 million (1996 census)
(Metropolitan): 16 million (2001 estimate)

Population Density
(City): 81,927 people per square mile (31,775 people per sq km)
(Metropolitan): 6,578 people per square mile (2,540 people per sq km)

suburbs to the west of the Nile are very different, with billboards advertising mobile phones and shops selling the latest in American and European fashions. Wealthy residential districts such as Zamalek are a world apart from the unplanned slums beneath the Muqattam Hills to the east. Cairo is a city of crowded markets and chaotic traffic, but also one of beautiful gardens, parks, and relaxing cafés.

Although dominated by Arabic-speaking Muslims, Cairo is a truly international city. Europeans, Americans, Africans, and people from many different cultures and religions live

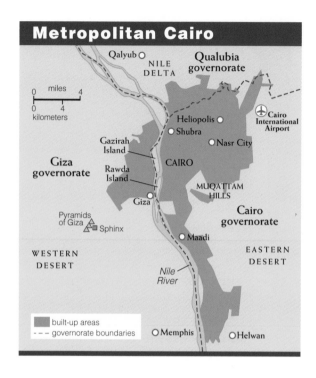

Metropolitan Cairo

▲ *Three administrative units, called governorates, together make up metropolitan Cairo. The most heavily populated of these is the Cairo governorate.*

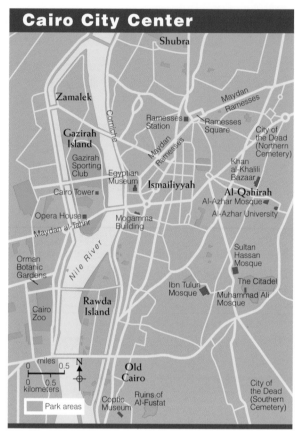

Cairo City Center

peacefully alongside one another. This makes Cairo an exciting city to explore and one that has attracted travelers for hundreds of years.

Geography
Cairo is located in the Nile River valley, just south of the Nile Delta. The city is very much the gift of the Nile, built along a narrow strip of fertile land to either side of the river. To the west lie the vast expanses of the Sahara Desert, while to the east the city is overlooked by the Muqattam Hills. Cairo's position at the junction of the Nile valley and delta has always given it great

control over these fertile farmlands. For centuries, the annual flooding of the Nile replenished the soils and made the land around Cairo some of the most fertile in the world. The Nile also provides a river connection between Cairo and the Mediterranean Sea 100 miles (160 km) to the north, which has long been important for bringing trade to the city.

Shaped to a large extent by the Nile, Greater Cairo stretches out along the river for more than 20 miles (32 km). In the south, it is hemmed in by the desert to either side, but farther north it spreads out as it nears the Nile delta.

▲ *The Nile River and central Cairo span the view from the Cairo Tower on the island of Gazirah.*

Cairo is the largest city on the African continent, but it is also politically, culturally, and geographically linked with the Middle East. It is a city where Africa and the Middle East join in a fascinating blend, unique in the world.

Greater Cairo

Egypt is divided into twenty-seven administrative units called governorates. The city of Cairo forms one of them, but the metropolitan area also includes parts of Qualubia and Giza governorates. Cairo governorate is at the heart of Greater Cairo on the east bank of the Nile and on two islands in the Nile called Rawdah and Gazirah. Cairo governorate is the business, education, and cultural center and the area of highest population density in Egypt. In parts of the city, there are more than 259,000 people per square mile (100,000 per sq km). Giza, west of the Nile, includes many of the newer residential areas and the world-famous pyramids. Qualubia governorate, to the north of the city, is mainly residential and industrial. Most people today refer to metropolitan Cairo simply as Cairo.

Climate

Cairo has a desert climate with just two seasons—a very hot summer and a cooler, but still warm, winter. Winter stretches from September through April. Temperatures can fall as low as 48° Farenheit (9° Celsius) in January and February but average about 68° F (20° C). Average temperatures during the summer months are about 80°F (27° C), but temperatures of over 104°F (40° C) are not uncommon. Cairo only receives about 1–2 inches (25–50 mm) of rain in a year, all of it falling during the winter. An unusual feature of Cairo's climate is a hot and dusty wind that blows in from the Sahara around April or May known as the khamsin. Its name comes from Arabic for "fifty" and refers to the fact that it often lasts for about fifty days.

CHAPTER 1

History of Cairo

The present-day site of Cairo dates back just over a thousand years, but the history of settlements in what is now the metropolitan region of Cairo dates back to ancient times. In the five thousand or so years that have passed since then, Cairo has undergone many transformations and had many different rulers. These have all contributed in their own way to make modern Cairo one of the most interesting and visited cities in the world.

The Pyramids of Giza

◄ *It was during the peak of Memphis's power that the pyramids of Giza (pictured left) were constructed by the ruling pharaohs of the time. The pyramids were built as burial chambers to secure the pharaohs' passages into the afterlife. To this day they remain the world's greatest stone buildings. No building since has ever used so much stone in its construction. The Great Pyramid of Cheops is made of an estimated 2.3 million blocks, each weighing about 2.5 tons (2.5 metric tons). It would have taken more than twenty thousand workers twenty years to build it. This amazing achievement is the only surviving member of the Seven Wonders of the World— a list of the wonders built by people of the ancient world that was first drawn up in the second century.*

"Man fears time, but time fears the pyramids."

—Arab proverb

Ancient Capital

Memphis, the oldest settlement in the region, was founded as the first capital of Egypt some time between 3000 B.C. and 2647 B.C. It was from Memphis that the early pharaohs (rulers of Ancient Egypt) began to build the great civilization that we now refer to as Ancient Egypt. Memphis remained the capital of Ancient Egypt until about 2100 B.C., when it was moved to Luxor further up the Nile. Although no longer the capital, Memphis continued to play an important role in Ancient Egypt as an administrative, commercial, and manufacturing center. Memphis still exists today on the southern outskirts of metropolitan Cairo, but little evidence remains of the original settlement.

Babylon and Al-Fustat

Power began to return to Cairo during the rule of the Persians (525–405 B.C.), when a canal was built between the Nile River and the Red Sea to the east. The canal joined the Nile opposite the island of Rawdah (today just south of downtown Cairo), and a new settlement developed here called Perhapemon, or Babylon as it became better known in Greek. (This settlement should not be confused with the more famous Babylon that was the capital of Babylonia in Mesopotamia.) Babylon remained an important military and trading settlement during the Greek and Roman periods of rule in Egypt (332–30 B.C. and 30 B.C.–A.D. 640, respectively), but their capital was in Alexandria to the north. It was not until the Arabs took control of Egypt in A.D. 641 that Cairo again became a capital—this time with the founding of Al-Fustat, a new settlement next to Babylon.

Al-Qahirah

In 969, the Fatimids (North African Arabs) gained control of Egypt and built a new capital, which they called Al-Qahirah, meaning "the subduer." Most consider this capital to be the origin of modern Cairo. Much of it is still clearly visible today, such as the Al-Azhar Mosque and Khan al-Khalili, Cairo's main *suq* (bazaar or market). Sections of the old city walls can still be seen. In the twelfth century, Fatamid control of Egypt was threatened by Christian

Misr

Al-Fustat grew rapidly as the Islamic empire, or caliphate, expanded into North Africa. Within just a few generations, it became a city of several hundred thousand people. The people living there called the city Misr, which is the Arabic name for Egypt, because it was the seat of the Egyptian government. To this day, Cairo is still known as Misr to Egyptians and other Arabic-speaking peoples.

▲ *The Citadel rests on a hill overlooking Cairo, an*
ideal place from which to govern the growing city.

Crusaders (European warriors who wanted
to replace Islamic rule with Christian rule)
and the Fatimids were forced to ask the
Syrian army for help in protecting the city.
The Syrians drove away the Crusaders but
then took control of the city themselves.

In 1171, a Kurdish general in the Syrian
army was placed in control of Cairo and
Egypt. He started a dynasty of rulers known
as the Ayyubids. His name was Salah Ad-din
Yusuf ibn Ayyub, or Saladin, as he was
known in the West. Saladin fortified Cairo

against further attacks from outside and
built one of its most famous landmarks—the
Citadel. This was a fortified settlement built
to enclose and protect the rulers of Egypt
together with their supporters and
assistants. It was from the Citadel that
important decisions were made, and it
remained the center of Egyptian
government for almost eight hundred years.

Ottoman Cairo

In 1250, Turkish slave soldiers, known as
Mamluks, overthrew the Ayyubid dynasty,
which they had served, and took control of
Cairo. They ruled the city until 1517, when

Egypt became a province of the Turkish Ottoman Empire. However, the Mamluks remained important during this period of Ottoman rule and continued to control daily life in Cairo and Egypt. In 1798, the Ottoman control of Cairo was interrupted by an invasion of French forces under the leadership of Napoleon Bonaparte. The French were not welcomed by the Egyptians, and in 1801 they were forced to withdraw.

By 1805, peace had returned to Egypt, and Cairo was under the control of an Ottoman army officer named Muhammad Ali. He began a long process of modernizing Egypt and Cairo, building new roads, introducing modern farming methods, and opening the country to foreigners and to tourism. He also rebuilt much of the Citadel and added the Muhammad Ali mosque, which dominates the skyline of eastern Cairo to this day. The modernization and growth of Cairo continued under Muhammad Ali's grandson Ismail, who was *khedive* (governor) of Egypt from 1863 to 1879.

▼ *The Sultan Hassan Mosque is a fine example of Mamluk architecture. Construction of the mosque began in 1356, and it took seven years to build.*

◀ *Cairenes celebrate the July 1952 revolution as Egyptian troops parade through the city.*

The British in Cairo

In 1882, the British took control of Egypt until Egypt could repay its debts to British and other European banks. The British based themselves in Cairo and built grand houses in districts such as Zamalek on Gazirah Island and Heliopolis in northeastern Cairo. The British allowed local rulers to stay but gave them little power to do anything. In 1919, opposition to British rule in Egypt led to riots on the streets of Cairo in which several hundred Cairenes and forty British soldiers were killed. By 1922, the British were forced to hand greater control back to the Egyptians, and King Fuad was made King of Egypt. In 1936, he was succeeded by his son, Farouk, who ruled until the Revolution of July 23, 1952, when he was forced to flee the country as military officers took control and declared Egypt a republic—a country to be ruled by elected leaders.

After the Revolution

Colonel Gamal Abdel Nasser emerged as the new leader of Egypt and was elected its first president in 1956. Under Nasser, Egypt was declared a socialist state, and all private companies and properties were nationalized for the benefit of the people. Thousands of foreigners left Cairo when their luxurious lifestyles were taken from them. It was about this time that Cairo began to expand

"Paris by the Nile"

During Ismail's reign, Cairo earned a reputation as "Paris by the Nile." This was because much of Cairo's growth at this time was based on designs and ideas that Ismail had brought back from France, where he had been educated. In particular, the new Ismailiyyah district of the city was built to resemble European cities of the time. This is now the downtown area of central Cairo, around Maydan al-Tahrir. Unfortunately, many of his large-scale projects were funded with loans from European banks that Ismail and Egypt soon found they could not repay.

rapidly as rural Egyptians rushed to the city to take advantage of the new government jobs that were being created. Services in the city were unprepared for this rapid growth, and, by the late 1960s, water, sewer, telephone, and other services were struggling to keep going.

▼ President Nasser's nationalization program caused rapid growth in Cairo's population as people moved to the city to work for the government.

Aswan High Dam

In 1960, work began on the construction of the Aswan High Dam across the Nile in the southern Nile valley. Its completion in 1970 meant that flooding on the Nile in Cairo was controlled for the first time in the city's history. This new certainty led to a massive expansion of the city on the western bank of the Nile, which had previously been flooded each year. New settlements sprang up and the city began a new phase of growth that is still continuing today.

Anwar Sadat succeeded Nasser in 1970 and began to reverse Egypt's socialist policies. He invited foreign companies to invest in Egypt and especially in Cairo. This policy, known as the *infetah*, or "open-door" policy, began to turn Cairo into the international city that it is today. In 1981, President Sadat was assassinated at a public celebration in Suez by Muslim fundamentalists (those who wanted the country to return to the religious and cultural basics of Islam) who were unhappy with Egypt's closer ties with western countries. He was succeeded by his vice president, Hosni Mubarak. President Mubarak now continues the process of making Cairo an international city and has overseen some of its most ambitious projects, such as a new Metro (subway) system and the development of satellite cities to house Cairo's growing population.

CHAPTER 2

People of Cairo

"There are but so many inhabitants, so much that the multitude [crowd] seems to move itself in waves, making the city appear . . . like a sea in perpetual agitation [motion]."

—Ibn Batuta, Arabic traveler, 1360.

Cairo has long been one of the most populated cities in the world, but in the last fifty years its population has grown extremely rapidly. This has made it difficult for city authorities to keep track of the exact population. Recent estimates of how many people live there vary from 10 to 20 million, depending on where the boundaries of the city are drawn. Cairo's population is still increasing rapidly and is likely to continue to do so for some time.

A Young Population

One reason for Cairo's continued population growth is the fact that more than half its inhabitants are estimated to be under the age of eighteen. Such a young population is common in mainly Islamic countries such as Egypt where there is a preference for large families. Many Islamic people are also against the use of contraceptives, which help

◄ *Cairo's streets are the center of life in the city and bustle with people at all hours of the day.*

to control population growth. As Cairo's children grow up and choose to start families of their own, they will probably add to the city population for many years to come.

Rural Migrants

In addition to internal population growth, thousands of newcomers arrive in Cairo every day. Most of them are *fellahin* (peasants) who come from Egypt's rural areas in the hope of finding a better life in Cairo. Young men are normally the first to arrive in the city in search of work. Once they have found a job and somewhere to live, they usually send for their families to join them in Cairo. Others leave their families behind and send money to them. There are several million fellahin now living in Cairo.

Outsiders

About 99 percent of Cairo's current population is made up of Egyptians, Bedouins, or Berbers. The Bedouins are originally a nomadic Arab people from Arabia and North Africa, while Berbers are a family of about twenty different ethnic groups found across North Africa. The remainder of the population includes people from a wide variety of different ethnic origins. Some of the main groups include Greeks, Nubians (from southern Egypt and northern Sudan), Armenians, Sudanese, Italians, and French. Cairo once had a substantial expatriate (foreign) community, but President Nasser expelled most foreigners following the revolution of 1952.

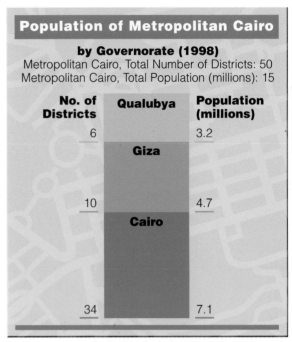

Population of Metropolitan Cairo

by Governorate (1998)
Metropolitan Cairo, Total Number of Districts: 50
Metropolitan Cairo, Total Population (millions): 15

No. of Districts	Qualubya / Giza / Cairo	Population (millions)
6	Qualubya	3.2
10	Giza	4.7
34	Cairo	7.1

Source: http://weekly.ahram.org.eg/2000/497/eg4.htm

Today, there are well over one hundred thousand expatriates (citizens from other countries) living in Cairo. In just one of Cairo's international schools, the six hundred pupils include children from more than fifty nationalities.

Religion

Cairo is an overwhelmingly Islamic city—its skyline is scattered with the minarets and domes of more than five hundred mosques. The mosques of Ibn Tulun, built in A.D. 879, Al-Azhar (970–972), and Muhammed Ali (1824–1857) are among the most famous and most visited in Cairo. About 90 percent of Cairo's population is Islamic, and most of these are Sunni Muslims—the main branch of the Islamic faith. Islam dominates city life in every way: from the clothes people wear

▲ Al-Azhar Mosque is the oldest in Cairo. Its university is the world's most important Islamic center of learning.

to the books and movies they enjoy and the way they behave. However, Islam in Egypt is not as strict as in some other Islamic countries. For example, women are a visible part of everyday Cairo life, whereas, in some Islamic countries, women are kept out of public view or wear veils to hide their faces.

Cairo's other main religion is Christianity, which accounts for roughly 10 percent of the population. Nearly all of Cairo's Christians are members of the Coptic Orthodox Church, a form of

"In the Islamic world, Cairo plays an extremely important role owing to the existence of Al-Azhar Mosque and University, which are the center of Islamic knowledge."

—Mahmoud Yousry and Tarek A. Aboul Atta, professor and associate professor at Cairo University.

Mawlid

A **mawlid** *marks the birthday of an Islamic shaykh (saint) respected for his wisdom or powers. People gather at the mausoleum (shrine) of the shaykh and perform a dance called the dhikr while chanting prayers. They believe that this will bring them closer to the shaykh and to God. There are close to one hundred mawlids celebrated in Cairo each year, some of them specific to certain neighborhoods. The biggest can attract more than two million pilgrims.*

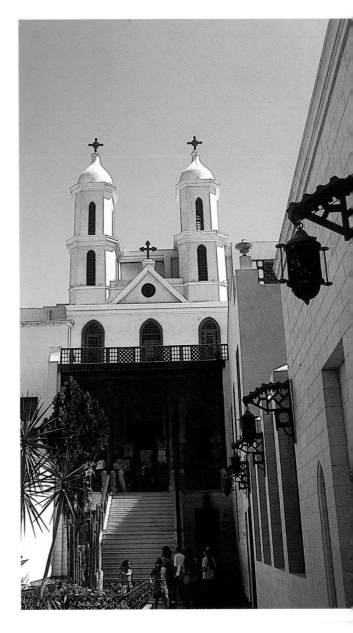

▶ *The Coptic Church of Saint Mary was built over the ruins of a gateway in a Roman fortress, so it has become known as Al-Muallaqah—the suspended, or hanging, church.*

Christianity that was founded in Alexandria, Egypt, well before the arrival of Islam. A following of about 150,000 Greek Orthodox Christians also lives in Cairo, and there are much smaller followings of other Christian denominations. Cairo also has three synagogues that serve its small Jewish community of about four hundred people.

Festivals

Most of Cairo's festivals are linked to the major religions of the city or to national days, such as July 23, which celebrates the 1952 revolution. For the Islamic community, the month of *Ramadan* is the most important event of the year. This month of fasting during daylight hours is followed by the three-day festival of *Id al-Fitr* (breaking of the fast). It is celebrated by visiting with relatives to enjoy great feasts and exchange presents. Ramadan occurs in the ninth month of the Islamic calendar. Because this calendar is made up of twelve lunar months (months that begin with the new moon),

▲ *Cairo's Muslims gather to celebrate* Id al-Adha
(the festival of sacrifice). This is marked seventy
days after the end of Ramadan by special prayers
and also with the sacrifice of an animal.

it is shorter—in terms of days—than the Western solar, or Gregorian, calendar (with its months of January, February, etc). Therefore, Ramadan, like other Islamic holidays, occurs on a different solar calendar date each year. Important dates for the Coptic Church include the Coptic New Year (September 11) and Epiphany, which is celebrated on January 6.

Food

Cairenes enjoy their food, and eating is a great social occasion, whether in a café or on the sidewalk, with food bought from one of Cairo's many street vendors. There is no

▲ Aysh *(bread) sellers are out early in the morning, selling Cairenes their staple food.*

one dish that could be said to be uniquely Cairene—instead, the cuisine is a mix of different influences from across the Middle East, Africa, and Europe. Bread is eaten with most meals. Its importance in the Cairene diet is represented in its local name *aysh*, which means "life." Among the most popular dishes in Cairo are *ful mudames* (fava bean stew), *kusheri* (pasta, rice, and lentils with a hot sauce), *mulukhiyyah* (a green leaf vegetable that is stewed with chicken or rabbit and served on rice), and *taamiya* (deep-fried beancakes also known as *felafel*). Cairenes commonly drink tea and coffee, and fresh fruit juices are popular when fruits are in season.

Like most modern cities, Cairo also has restaurants that offer foods from around the world, including French, Italian, and Asian cuisines. Many of the restaurants are too expensive for the average Cairene, however, and are more often visited by the wealthier tourists and expatriates living in Cairo.

CHAPTER 3

Living in Cairo

"Cairenes have the ability to feel cozy in conditions of noisiness and overcrowding that a Westerner would regard as intolerable."

—Max Rodenbeck, author, *Cairo, The City Victorious*, 1998.

The pressure of Cairo's massive population is felt throughout the city. Its roads are congested, its housing is overcrowded, trash is everywhere, and pollution fills the air. There are, of course, the leafy suburbs, where it is possible to escape all this, but they are few and are reserved for Cairo's elite—the small group of Egyptians and expatriates who enjoy highly paid jobs. The majority of Cairenes must face the daily challenges of living in an overpopulated city. Despite this, most go about their daily lives with a remarkable amount of happiness and good humor. There is a strong sense of connection to the community, and many believe that this has helped to limit problems such as crime and violence that often occur in cities with such enormous social divisions.

◄ *No space is wasted in Cairo, and many people live in apartments above the city's shops.*

▲ In suburbs such as Zamalek on the island of Gazirah, wealthy Cairenes live in large houses, many of which were built during British rule.

"People stay in [downtown] Cairo because it has spirit. Thousands of years of dwelling has created a pattern of relationships that is very valuable."

—Abdel Halim, Cairene architect, 1996.

Most people in Cairo live in apartments, many of which have been extended upward to deal with the growing population. They have nearly all been built within the last fifty years and are often arranged around a central courtyard. A middle-class family typically lives in an apartment that consists of a kitchen, bathroom, family room, and one or two bedrooms. In the poorer parts of Cairo, however, families may have only a single large room and must cook and bathe outside. Individual houses (known as villas) are only found in the wealthier parts of the city, such as Heliopolis and Maadi (on the southern edge of Cairo). These are similar to typical houses found in the United States or Europe and are home to expatriates working in Cairo or to wealthy Egyptians.

Housing

Cairo was never planned to cope with the huge number of people who live there today, and as a result, housing is in short supply. One of the major difficulties is that there is no land left in the city for building new housing. With every available space used up, housing in Cairo has been divided up into smaller and smaller units.

Satellite Cities

The government is encouraging people to move out of the city center to new satellite cities in the deserts surrounding Cairo. Many Cairenes, however, are reluctant to leave their friends and families behind, so in some satellite cities, apartment buildings remain empty. Those built on the edge of the city rather than away from Cairo have been

Cities of the Dead

The most famous slums in Cairo are the Cities of the Dead—two vast Muslim cemeteries in the east of the city. The tombs in these cemeteries are permanent structures (pictured below) with rooms organized around a central courtyard. It has always been normal for a relative to live in the tomb to care for it and to protect the dead. Over time, though, whole families have moved into these tombs, and squatters have occupied those with no family already living in them. Estimates of the population vary, but it is believed that more than 250,000 people now live and work in and among the tombs. There are schools, stores, and bus stops to meet the needs of the tomb dwellers.

more successful. They include May 15 City south of Helwan and also Salam City and Nasr City in the area around Cairo Airport.

Slum housing

Since the 1960s, about two-thirds of the new housing built in Cairo has been informal (unplanned and unofficial). Such housing is often referred to as slum housing, and estimates suggest that between one- and two-thirds of Cairo's population lives in

"We have found openness and eagerness on the part of poor communities to send their girls to school if it is free of charge and close to home."

—Malak Zaalouk, United Nation's Children's Fund (UNICEF) education officer in Cairo, 2000.

such slums. Slum housing is normally built to poor standards using whatever materials are available. These houses rarely have electricity, water, or sewers and normally lack services such as schools, hospitals, and transportation. Over time, some of the slums have become fully established neighborhoods, and the government has been forced to provide some services.

Education in Cairo

The basic education system in Cairo starts when children are six years of age and consists of five years of elementary school and three years of preparatory school. At the end of this time, students are given the Basic Education Completion Certificate. Basic education is compulsory and state funded, but not all children go to school. Some parents cannot afford the extra expenses such as uniforms, textbooks, and stationery. Other parents keep their children from school to help out around the home or send them out to find paid work. This is particularly true for girls, whose education is not always valued in Islamic societies. In Cairo (and in Egypt in general), however, more girls are attending

▲ *Children gather each morning before school to raise the Egyptian flag and sing the national anthem.*

school every year as their parents realize the benefits of education.

At age fourteen, children can choose to attend either a general secondary school or a technical secondary school. Secondary school pupils usually study academic subjects for three years and then take exams that lead to *Thanaweya a' Amma* (General Secondary Education Certificate (GSEC).

23

▶ *The spices of Suq al-Attarin provide a colorful and beautifully scented shopping experience.*

Courses at a technical secondary school include training in business, industry, or agriculture. They normally last for three or five years and lead to a Technical Diploma.

University Education

Cairo has several universities and is a major center of learning. Cairo University alone has more than 155,000 students, while Ain Shams University (near Heliopolis) has 130,000. Cairo's most famous university is the Islamic university of Al-Azhar in Al-Qahirah. It was founded in A.D. 970 and is said to be the oldest university in the world. It was originally a center for Islamic studies but now teaches a wide range of additional courses. Al-Azhar is smaller than Cairo's other universities but is very prestigious and attracts Muslims from around the world.

"With a character all of its own, Khan al-Khalili is exactly what an oriental bazaar should be and more. It is laden with various kinds of goods, crowded with tourists, craftsmen, and local people, and filled with exotic odors."

—Robert Morkot, Egyptologist and author, *Egypt*, 1997.

Shopping in Cairo

Cairenes have a great choice of places to shop. As in most major cities around the world, Cairo has large department stores and supermarkets as well as many stores that specialize in selling particular

Khan al-Khalili

Most visitors to Cairo will at some point visit Khan al-Khalili, one of the largest markets in the world. Located in the historic Al-Qahira district, it is now mainly a tourist market offering typical Cairene and Egyptian wares as well as more tacky tourist souvenirs. Gold and silver jewelry, gemstones, copper and brassware, leather goods, cotton, perfumes, carpets, and rugs are all for sale. There are no fixed prices, and tourists are expected to haggle for the best price. This can be a fun and exciting experience, but the traders know every trick in the book, and shoppers have to work hard to get a real bargain.

goods, such as electrical items, books, gifts, or antiques. Overall, independent, small shops (some of which have been run by the same family for generations) continue to dominate Cairo.

The most unique shopping experience that Cairo has to offer is to be found at the suqs (bazaars or markets), most of which are found in Al-Qahirah—the original heart of Cairo. Khan al-Khalili is the largest and best known of them, but there are many others organized according to what they sell. Suq al-Sagha, for example, is the goldsmiths' market where Cairene women buy their gold and silver jewelry. Suq Nahhasin is the coppersmiths' market, while at Suq al-Attarin an incredible range of spices, herbs, roots, and seeds are beautifully displayed in large, open sacks.

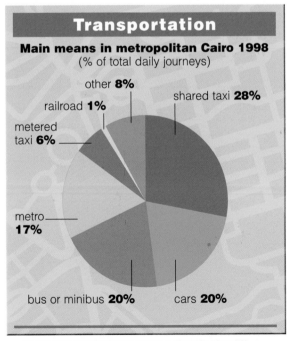

Transportation

Main means in metropolitan Cairo 1998
(% of total daily journeys)

other **8%**
railroad **1%**
metered taxi **6%**
shared taxi **28%**
metro **17%**
bus or minibus **20%**
cars **20%**

Source: World Bank Urban Transport Strategy Review: The Case of Cairo, Egypt, 2000

October 6 Bridge

One of the most important transportation structures in Cairo is the October 6 Bridge. The bridge section stretches across the Nile and connects downtown Cairo to the island of Gazirah. The majority of the structure is actually a raised highway stretching eastward into the heart of Cairo for a distance of about 12 miles (20 km). The bridge was started in 1969 and was completed in 1996. Now known as the spinal cord of Cairo, it carries about half of the city's vehicle traffic every day—an estimated forty thousand vehicles.

Getting Around

Cairo is a city that seems to be constantly on the move. For short distances, most people walk, but for anything longer they normally rely on public transportation. Buses and minibuses, one of the main forms of transportation, serve all parts of the city from the central bus station in Maydan al-Tahrir. Traveling by bus is cheap but often extremely crowded, so those who can afford them prefer taxis, and shared taxis, where passengers also share costs, are particularly popular. Many wealthier residents buy their own cars, but with more than 2 million cars already on Cairo's roads, these simply add to congestion and pollution problems. Water taxis that run both across as well as up and down the Nile are one way to escape the heavy traffic of the city streets, but they can also be very crowded.

▲ Cairo's streets were not built to handle the amount of traffic the city now has. It is one of the world's most congested cities.

In 1987, the first stretch of a new Metro subway line was opened in Cairo to try to relieve congestion in the city. Two lines are now completed, stretching for about 40 miles (65 km) and carrying more than 2 million passengers a day. One line runs from El-Marg in the northeast through the center of the city and then to Helwan, south of Cairo. The other line runs from the northern parts of the city to the center, continuing southwest to Giza. Four more lines are planned by 2025 to connect to other parts of the city and the new satellite cities. The metro is a clean, efficient, and inexpensive transportation system.

"Only the fit and the young braved the terrific congestion of Cairo's buses, which careered through the city with men hanging from their doors and windows like barnacles."

—Stanley Stewart, travel writer, *Old Serpent Nile*, 1991.

Center of Rail and Air

The Metro subway system is run by Egyptian State Railways, which also runs trains to most major cities in Egypt. Cairo lies at the center of this railroad system, and trains depart from the enormous Ramesses station, off Maydan Ramesses. Cairo International Airport, about 15 miles (24 km) northeast from the center of Cairo, serves as the main entry point for tourists visiting Egypt. The government-run airline, EgyptAir, operates domestic flights from this airport as well.

▲ Smog hangs over Cairo in the morning light. Poor air quality is a major cause of ill health for Cairenes.

Environmental Concerns

Cairo faces several environmental concerns, but by far the most serious issue is air pollution. According to the World Health Organization (WHO), air pollution in the city can be up to one hundred times higher than levels that are considered safe. This makes Cairo's air some of the most polluted in the world, and it is thought to cause up

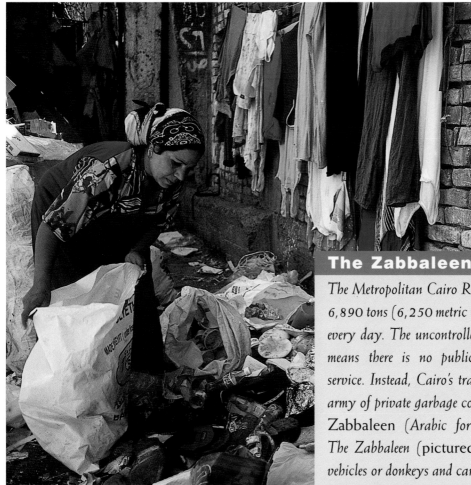

to twenty-five thousand deaths a year. The main sources of air pollution are emissions from Cairo's industries and from poorly maintained vehicles. In 1997, the Cairo Air Improvement Project (CAIP) was launched to try to reduce levels of air pollution. One of its first steps was to introduce unleaded gasoline. This reduced lead pollution in Cairo's air by 88 percent in just one year. CAIP is also working with local industries to try and reduce their emissions into the environment.

The Zabbaleen

The Metropolitan Cairo Region generates about 6,890 tons (6,250 metric tons) of solid garbage every day. The uncontrolled growth of the city means there is no public garbage collection service. Instead, Cairo's trash is collected by an army of private garbage collectors known as the Zabbaleen (Arabic for garbage collector). The Zabbaleen (pictured above) use motor vehicles or donkeys and carts to collect the waste from apartments and slums across Cairo. They then return to their neighborhood beneath the Muqattam Hills, where the trash is carefully sorted. Organic material (food scraps and vegetables, and so on) is fed to pigs, while nonorganic trash is sorted into its different types, such as plastics, glass, paper, copper, aluminum, and clothing. Once sorted, the trash is sold for recycling or as raw material. The Zabbaleen recycle an estimated 80 percent of the garbage that they collect and make a vital contribution to garbage management in Cairo.

CHAPTER 4

Cairo at Work

Cairo is an industrious and bustling city. Everywhere, people go about their daily business from daybreak until late into the night. Cairenes are hardworking people, and many struggle to make any kind of living at all. Unemployment is a problem in Cairo because there are simply not enough jobs to keep up with the population.

The Informal Economy

Cairo has a large informal economy. This is made up of people who create their own incomes by selling goods or offering services and by people who find short-term work for which they are paid by the day. Workers in many of the more visible jobs in Cairo, such as shoe-shiners, laborers, market porters, craftspeople, and street vendors, are part of this informal economy. Such work is known as informal because people are not officially employed and do not pay taxes on their income. Some experts believe that up to 90 percent of Cairo's economy is in the informal sector.

Industrial Heart

Cairo is the economic heart of Egypt. It is home to nearly all of Egypt's major banks and businesses and has about half of its

◀ *These men are helping unload building materials. Short-term work such as this is typical of Cairo's informal economy, providing wages but not security.*

Baksheesh

Wages in Cairo are very low compared to those in North America or Europe, and most people would find it hard to survive on their official salaries alone. A system of tipping, called baksheesh, *helps to supplement their incomes. In western countries, tipping is normally used in restaurants or perhaps for a taxi driver, but in Cairo baksheesh is paid by everyone and for everything. Parking the car, opening a door, getting the freshest vegetables at the market, even being shown to a movie theater seat—all of this requires a little baksheesh. Many of the lowest-paid workers, such as hotel or office cleaners, rely on baksheesh for most of their income.*

▲ *A traditional craftsman uses age-old techniques to make patterns in a copper plate.*

industries. Food processing, textiles, steel and iron works, chemicals, and construction are among the most important industries in Cairo. There are also factories that manufacture items such as cars, refrigerators, and a wide range of domestic goods. The main industrial areas of Cairo are to the north and south of the city in the districts of Shubra and Helwan. In recent years, the Egyptian government has been trying to encourage industries to move to the new satellite cities around the edge of Cairo. For example, there are lower rates of tax if businesses move to the new settlements.

Child Labor

◄ *Many traditional industries in Cairo employ children as a major part of their workforce. It has been estimated that, in Cairo's leather tanneries, 25 percent of the workers are children whose average age is eleven. Some of them work for their own families, but others may work for strangers to earn money for their families. Children also work in nontraditional industries, such as restaurants and shops, and some are sent out to beg for money on the streets.*

This helps to provide jobs for the people moving there while also helping reduce pollution and congestion in the city center.

Traditional Industries

A wide range of traditional industries still thrives in Cairo, especially in the older parts of the city. Leather tanning, metalwork, carpentry, and tailoring are particularly important and are often centered on Cairo's famous bazaars or markets. The skills needed for these industries have been passed down over hundreds of years, often within the same family. Some of the techniques used today have changed little since the time of the pharaohs.

Government Workers

The Egyptian government, which is based in Cairo, is a major employer in the city. According to some estimates, more than 1 million people work in government departments and offices across the city. There are so many government employees that they have even been given their own social class, known as the *muwazzafin*. The Mogamma building in Maydan al-Tahrir is the most famous government building. It accommodates about eighteen thousand workers. More than fifty thousand people visit the Mogamma every day, and it has became famous for its long lines and slow service. Egyptians must go there to apply for licenses or to have official forms stamped and approved, but even the simplest tasks can involve a piece of paper going to several departments and being seen by many different people.

Working Women

In most other mainly Islamic cities, women do not normally have jobs but instead look after the home and provide for the family. In Cairo, however, low wages mean that men often earn too little to support their families, and so women must also look for paid work. Most of the jobs done by women are in offices, and about 70 percent of Cairo's working women are employed in one of the many government departments. Unlike some Islamic cities, in Cairo, women can also be found doing more skilled and professional jobs, and the city has many female doctors, dentists, teachers, lawyers, and engineers. A major problem that Cairo's working women face is that they must also

▲ *Thousands of Cairenes work for the government. These workers are standing outside the Mogamma building in Maydan al-Tahrir.*

Nasser's Promise

When Gamal Abdel Nasser became president of Egypt in 1956, he promised all university graduates in Egypt a job for life. Thousands of new jobs were created in government offices, but many of them were of little importance, and most were very poorly paid. Now, because of this, many of Cairo's workers are listed on a government payroll even if there is actually no job for them to do. Many of these workers have found different jobs or run their own businesses.

perform their traditional roles of looking after the home and caring for the family. This means Cairene women work extremely long hours and have very little leisure time compared to men.

Foreign Investment
In 1974, Egypt adopted a new economic policy called infetah, meaning "open-door." This policy encouraged overseas companies to set up offices and factories in Egypt and to invest in the Egyptian economy. International businesses soon began arriving

▲ *The Mena House Oberoi Hotel is one of Cairo's best, with spectacular views of the pyramids at Giza —one of the world's greatest tourist attractions.*

in Egypt, and most of them located in Cairo. It rapidly became a major global city as it provided a gateway for U.S. and European businesses to find new markets for their goods in Africa and the Middle East. Today, Cairo remains the most important economic center in the Middle East, and international companies are still investing in the city. There are now banks, car showrooms, shops, businesses, and fast food restaurants from around the world, many of them internationally famous.

Tourism

One of the fastest growing industries in Cairo is tourism. Egypt receives nearly 6 million tourists each year, most of whom arrive in, or spend some time in, Cairo. Tourism is the biggest earner of foreign revenue in Egypt. The most obvious attractions for tourists are the pyramids at Giza on the western edge of the city and the Egyptian Museum in the center of Cairo. Khan al-Khalili and the Citadel are also popular with visitors. Tourism provides people with numerous job opportunities in Cairo. Many serve as drivers or hotel porters or as souvenir sellers or city guides. Many more people benefit from the income tourism brings to the city; in fact, it is now one of Cairo's main sources of income.

National Government

As the capital of the country, Cairo is home to the national government of Egypt. This is led by President Hosni Mubarak, who has been in power since 1981. Egypt is a multiparty democracy but is dominated by the ruling National Democratic Party (NDP). The NDP has strong links with the Egyptian military, whose power is sometimes used to keep control of the country.

A candidate for president is nominated by the People's Assembly, a body of 350 or more elected members, and then the candidate is voted into a six-year term of office by public referendum. A president may serve for an unlimited number of terms of office. The president has the power to appoint vice presidents, ministers, and the prime minister. The People's Assembly is needed to approve government policy, the national budget, and all laws.

Several Islamic fundamentalist groups would like to overthrow the government and see Egypt become a more Islamic state. They have been fighting a war of terrorism against the government since 1992, and Cairo has often been a target for their attacks. In 1997, a bus bomb killed nine German tourists at the Egyptian museum in the heart of the city. Increased fear of terrorism has hurt both tourism and foreign investment in Cairo, as it has in many other cities around the world.

Local Government

Egypt is divided into administrative units called governorates, each led by a governor appointed by the central government, which maintains tight control over local government. Each governorate is further divided into districts and villages. At each level, an elected council works with appointed officials to address issues of public services, housing, agriculture, education, and health. Cairo is one of five Egyptian cities that have governorate status. Its metropolitan area has grown so much that its region now includes parts of two other governorates.

CHAPTER 5

Cairo at Play

In a city as noisy and busy as Cairo, it seems impossible that people could ever relax and enjoy their own leisure time. Yet Cairo offers many ways for people to enjoy themselves, from grand productions of opera or ballet to simple pleasures such as walking along the Nile or relaxing with friends in one of the city's many *ahwas* (coffee houses). There are also areas around Cairo where people like to escape the city on day trips or longer breaks. Cairo is a city and society where close contacts with the family are very important, so Cairenes spend a large amount of their spare time visiting their families.

Open Spaces

For millions of Cairenes, the cost of leisure and entertainment in the city is simply too high. This does not stop them, though, from enjoying themselves, and Cairenes make good use of what little open space there is in the city. Parks and gardens are popular for walking, while any open space is used by children for playing soccer, riding a bike, or skating. A particularly popular area is the waterfront and gardens of Gazirah— the island in the middle of the Nile. The Orman Botanic Gardens and Cairo

◀ *In such a crowded city, space for children to play is extremely limited. This swing is in the grounds of the fourteenth-century Muaayyad Mosque.*

> *"The amount of green space per citizen [in Cairo] has been calculated at thirteen square centimeters, not enough to cover a child's palm."*
>
> —Dan Richardson, *Rough Guide to Egypt*, 2003.

Zoo (both in Giza) are also popular open spaces, while the Corniche along the east bank of the Nile is a favorite place for an evening walk.

The Ahwa

The place where most Cairenes go to relax and socialize is the local ahwa. These coffee houses are the center of the community in

Sheesha

In most of Cairo's ahwas, people enjoy smoking flavored tobacco using a type of pipe known as a sheesha. This is a water pipe in which the tobacco smoke is filtered by water in a glass bowl. A sheesha is very different from a cigarette because it does not have the harmful chemicals of most cigarettes and uses a relatively small amount of tobacco, which is normally mixed with molasses or apple to give it flavor. The sheesha has been a part of Arabic culture for hundreds of years.

▼ Fishawi *is the most famous ahwa in Cairo. It is always busy with people enjoying coffee, a cold drink, or a sheesha pipe.*

▲ *A movie poster advertises one of the new releases. Since people today increasingly own televisions and videos, moviegoing is becoming less popular.*

Cairo—places where people meet to catch up on news, to share ideas, to discuss current affairs, and to play games. *Domina* (dominoes) and *towla* (backgammon) are the most popular games, but cards and chess are also played. In some ahwas, Cairenes can find traditional storytellers repeating age-old tales that are often set to music. Traditionally, only men went to ahwas, but now that women have become more a part of public life, women also enjoy stopping in these coffee houses. Coffee and tea are the traditional beverages served in an ahwa, but today many cold beverages are also available. These include *karkaday*, a delicious beverage made from hibiscus blossoms. Cairo's most famous ahwa is Fishawi in Khan al-Khalili. Open twenty-four hours a day, it claims to have never closed since 1773.

The Movies

Cairenes are enthusiastic moviegoers, and there are many movie theaters in the metropolitan Cairo area for them to choose from. Cairo also has its own movie industry. In fact, between the 1960s and mid-1980s, Cairo produced about one hundred movies a year. Movies made in Cairo were shown across the Arabic-speaking world, but the industry is now in decline and only produces about ten movies a year. The main reasons for this decline are an increase in government tax on movie tickets and greater private ownership of televisions and videos. This means that many Cairenes no longer visit the theaters as often as they used to. There has also been an increase in imported movies, especially from the United States, so that most movie theaters now show a mix of foreign and local movies. All movies in Cairo are strictly censored to make sure they do not offend Islamic values.

Sufi Dancers

Sufism is a branch of Islam in which people believe they can get closer to God by chanting and spinning in a rhythmic dance known as Sufi dancing (pictured below). Also known as whirling dervishes, Sufi dancers perform two public shows a week in Cairo. These shows are mainly for tourists today, but Sufi dancing is still practiced and enjoyed by followers of Sufism.

Opera, Dance, and Theater

Ballet, modern dance, and opera are all popular entertainment in Cairo, but ticket prices mean that often only the wealthier can afford to attend. The opera house, where most performances are staged, is on

Gazhirah Island and was built in the 1980s. Theater performances are more widely enjoyed. Indoor and outdoor performances take place across the city. Comedy is among the most popular forms of theater, but, as with movies, all performances are censored by the authorities. Cairo is particularly famous for its belly dancing clubs. The belly dance, or *raqs sharqi* (oriental dance) as it is properly known, is a form of female dancing and singing that involves exaggerated hip and belly movements. Cairo's top belly dancers live in luxurious mansions and are treated the way movie stars are in the United States.

Sporting Cairo

The most widely followed sport in Cairo is soccer. Young boys can be seen all over the city practicing their soccer skills in the hope of one day playing on the same team as their sporting heroes. The city's two main teams are Zamalek and Ahli, and their matches are attended by thousands of loyal supporters. In fact, soccer is so popular that when these matches are played, Cairo's streets become quiet.

The Nile is used as a sports venue by about ten rowing clubs based in Cairo. They practice on the river and hold competitions every Friday between November and April. Cairo also has two popular nine-hole golf courses and a horse racetrack in Heliopolis, where there are regular weekend races.

Leaving the City

If Cairenes wish to escape the hustle and bustle of the city, they normally head for Alexandria on the Mediterranean coast north of Cairo. This city is especially popular during the hot summers when it is several degrees cooler than Cairo and has refreshing breezes that blow in from the sea. Wealthier Cairenes may even have a second home in Alexandria, where they stay for the summer months. Most people, however, just visit for the day, taking one of the many buses or trains that make the two- to three-hour journey daily. The beaches to the west of Alexandria are the main attraction, but walking along the Corniche (the coastal road) or relaxing in a seafront café are also popular pastimes.

The Egyptian Museum

◀ *Cairo is home to the Egyptian Museum, which, with exhibits that cover all of Egypt's long history, is one of the finest museums in the world. It is said that if you looked at each of its more than 100,000 exhibits for one minute, it would take nine months to get around. The most famous exhibits are the 1,700 treasures of the boy pharaoh Tutankhamun. Discovered in 1922 in the Valley of the Kings in Luxor, Egypt, by the British archaeologist Howard Carter, they include Tutankhamun's famous death mask (pictured left), which is made of solid gold inlaid with precious stones.*

CHAPTER 6

Looking Forward

> *"Life is what this city is about . . . only a person who's tired of life itself could fail to see the charm of Cairo."*
>
> —Andrew Humphreys, author,
> *Lonely Planet Guide to Cairo*, 2002.

Many great challenges face Cairo as it enters the twenty-first century. At the center of many of these challenges is the city's continued population growth. Between three and four hundred thousand children are born in Cairo every year and this places enormous pressure on housing, transportation, education, health care, and other services that are already stretched to their limits. In addition, Cairo is still receiving immigrants from Egypt's rural areas and other urban centers every day. In 2000, it was estimated that one-quarter of Egypt's population was living in Cairo.

Cost of Living

One of the biggest problems facing Cairenes has been the gradual removal of government subsidies from many parts of their lives. The government has been subsidizing (artificially making cheaper) basic needs such as food, housing,

◄ *The October 6 Bridge commemorates a 1973 attack, ultimately unsucccessful, on Israel. It now links Central Cairo with Gazirah Island.*

transportation, education, health care, and even entertainment in Cairo since the 1960s. These subsidies used to help make life more manageable for the millions of Cairenes living on low incomes, but they were also costing the government a great deal of money. In 1991, the government launched a series of economic reforms that have involved privatizing (selling to private owners) state-owned companies and reducing or removing state subsidies. For wealthy Cairenes, this has brought many new opportunities, but for millions of others, it has meant higher living costs and greater poverty.

Positive Steps

Although Cairo has problems to overcome, it has made positive steps in recent years. The new subway system is among its proudest achievements. Many Cairenes happily boast that it is the first subway system in Africa. There have also been reductions in Cairo's appalling pollution that are making the city a more pleasant place to live. Cairo has succeeded in attracting new businesses to the city and in encouraging more tourists to visit. Those arriving in the city today see a city that has not only a fascinating past but also a positive and exciting future as one of the world's greatest cities.

▶ *Cairo's expanding subway system is an efficient form of underground transportation that helps relieve traffic congestion in the overcrowded city.*

A Divided City

There is a growing gap between the rich and poor in Cairo, and some experts are concerned that this could lead to future troubles. They are particularly worried that Cairo's youth might become frustrated and angry at the lack of opportunities and the rising costs of living. When food subsidies were last reduced, in 1977, major riots known as the "bread riots" took place on the streets of Cairo as people protested about growing inequality. The government wants to avoid the repeat of any such riots in the future.

Time Line

c. 3000 B.C. Memphis is founded as the early capital of Ancient Egypt.

c. 2500 B.C. The pyramids are built at Giza.

c. 2100 B.C. The capital of Egypt is moved from Memphis to Luxor.

A.D. 641 Al-Fustat is founded as the new capital of Arab-controlled Egypt.

969 The Fatimids of North Africa invade Egypt and establish a new capital called Al-Qahirah (modern day Cairo).

1171 Saladin becomes the ruler of Egypt and founds the Ayyubid dynasty. In 1176, he begins the construction of the Citadel.

1250 The Mamluks, Turkish slave soldiers, overthrow the Ayyubid dynasty and take control of Cairo.

1517 Cairo and Egypt become part of the Turkish Ottoman Empire.

1798–1801 Egypt is invaded and occupied by France, which is then forced to withdraw.

1805–1848 Mohammad Ali the Great begins the modernization of Cairo.

1863–1879 Ismail, the grandson of Muhammad Ali, turns Cairo into the "Paris of the Nile," going into debt to the British.

1882 The British take control of Cairo and Egypt.

1919 There are riots in Cairo in protest against continued British rule.

1922 King Fuad becomes the first king of Egypt, but the British remain in control.

1936 King Farouk succeeds his father.

1952 Army officers oust the king and declare Egypt a republic.

1956 Gamal Abdel Nasser becomes the first president of Egypt.

1967 June 10 Israel launches a preemptive war on Egypt, Jordan, and Syria.

1970 Anwar Sadat succeeds Nasser as president of Egypt. The Aswan High Dam is completed so western Cairo can develop.

1973 October 6 Egypt and Syria invade Israel. Egypt ultimately gains control of the Suez Canal, and Syria regains some pre-1967 territory.

1974 President Sadat begins the infetah, or "open door" economic policy.

1981 Sadat is assassinated and succeeded by President Hosni Mubarak.

1992 An earthquake strikes Cairo and kills at least five hundred people.

1997 A terrorist bomb kills tourists outside the Egyptian Museum.

1999 President Mubarak wins his fourth term as president.

2003 March 21 Cairene antiwar protesters join world-wide demonstrations against the U.S. invasion of Iraq; many are arrested.

Glossary

ahwa Arabic word for coffee or a coffee house, which is Cairo's equivalent of a café.

Arab League an organization (formed in 1945 to promote unity and cooperation) made up of twenty-one Arab states.

baksheesh money given as a tip or a bribe in order to get something done. Baksheesh is common throughout the Middle East.

Cairene the name used to describe a person or people who live in the city of Cairo.

commuter a person who travels to work in the city from a home that is in the suburbs or an outlying area.

crusaders warriors from Europe who undertook several missions between the eleventh and thirteenth centuries to forcibly convert Muslim countries to Christianity.

Coptic Orthodox Church the main Christian church of Egypt, founded in about 43 A.D.

delta a wide triangular-shaped region at the end of a river where the water slows, causing the river to deposit its sediment and add to the area before it enters the sea.

dhikr a dance performed at a mawlid festival in the belief that it will bring people closer to their saints and to God.

dynasty a series of rulers from one family.

Epiphany in the Coptic Orthodox tradition, a celebration of the baptism of Christ.

expatriate a person who lives abroad.

Fatimids an Arabic people from North Africa who seized control of Egypt in the tenth century and founded the modern city of Cairo.

governorate an administrative division/district in Egypt. There are twenty-six governorates in Egypt, and metropolitan Cairo includes parts of three of them.

Islam the religion followed by Muslims. It is based on the seventh-century teachings of Muhammad, who is believed to be the Prophet of God by his followers. Islam is the world's second-largest religion.

Islamic fundamentalists Muslims who want to return to the basics of Islam and reject modern influences.

Mamluks Turkish slave soldiers who seized control of Egypt from the Ayyubid dynasty in A.D. 1250.

mawlid a festival/celebration held to commemorate the birthday of an Islamic saint known as a shayk.

maydan a small, circular plaza.

nationalized brought into the control of the national government instead of being owned, operated, and managed by private individuals or companies.

Ottoman describes the Turkish people that formed an empire and once controlled large parts of the Middle East, including Egypt.

pharaoh the title given to rulers of Ancient Egypt.

pyramids stone structures built by Ancient Egyptians as burial places for their pharaohs.

Glossary

socialist state a state that follows the principles of socialism, whereby the government controls the means of production and distribution in order to share their benefits fairly and equally among the population.

subsidies government monetary support given to help maintain specific groups.

suq Arabic for a market or bazaar. It is sometimes also spelled as *souq* or *souk*.

Sunni Muslim the main branch of the Islamic faith. Sunni Muslims follow the beliefs of the Sunna—a set of Islamic laws based on the words and deeds of Muhammad, the Prophet of Islam.

Further Information

Books

Joan D. Barghusen. *Daily Life in Ancient and Modern Cairo.*
Lerner Publishing Group, 2001.

Andrew Humphreys. *Cairo.*
Lonely Planet Publications, 2002.

Fiona MacDonald. *Tutankhamen.*
Chelsea House, 2000.

John Rodenbeck (ed). *Insight Guide Cairo* (*Insight Guides*).
Langenscheidt Publishers, 1998.

R. Conrad Stein. *Cairo.*
Children's Press, 1996.

Florence Parry Heide. *The Day of Ahmed's Secret.*
Lothrop, Lee & Shepard, 1990.

Web Sites

www.cairotourist.com/
Learn more from the official Egyptian ministry of tourism Web page for Cairo.

www.egyptianmuseum.gov.eg/
Discover the treasures of Cairo's Egyptian Museum.

home.att.net/~cairo3dmap/map.html
Zoom in and explore a three-dimensional map of Cairo.

inic.utexas.edu/menic/cairo/
Examine a U.S.-based educational Web site about the history and future of Cairo.

www.lonelyplanet.com/destinations/ africa/cairo/
Gain good background information about Cairo.

www.touregypt.net/cairo1.htm
Gather more information on visiting Cairo.

Index

MAY 2 2 2009

31^{oo}